The Business of Listening

Become a more effective listener

Fourth Edition

Diane Bonet Romero

A Crisp Fifty-Minute™ *Series Book*

AXZO PRESS

The Business of Listening

Become a more effective listener

Fourth Edition

Diane Bonet Romero

CREDITS:

President, Axzo Press:	**Jon Winder**
Vice President, Product Development:	**Charles G. Blum**
Vice President, Operations:	**Josh Pincus**
Director, Publishing Systems Development:	**Dan Quackenbush**
Developmental Editor:	**Steve English**
Copy Editor:	**Ken Maher**

Trademarks

Crisp Fifty-Minute Series is a trademark of Axzo Press.

Some of the product names and company names used in this book have been used for identification purposes only and may be trademarks or registered trademarks of their respective manufacturers and sellers.

Disclaimer

We reserve the right to revise this publication and make changes from time to time in its content without notice.

ISBN 10: 1-4260-1848-7
ISBN 13: 978-1-4260-1848-0
Printed in the United States of America
1 2 3 4 5 6 7 8 9 10 12 11 10 09

Table of Contents

About the Author

Although she's now retired, Diana Bonet Romero devoted her 25-year career to developing and conducting seminars in business writing, technical writing, and listening skills. Ms. Romero was one of the first 100 members of the International Listening Association when it began in the late 1970s. Her client list included major corporations and government agencies in the United States, Canada, and Europe.

Presently, Ms. Romero lives with her husband in Northern California, where she continues her work. She also acts as a writing coach for new writers and enjoys freelance editing assignments. In her free time, she's an avid reader and gardener, depending on the weather.

Other books by Ms. Romero include *Clear Writing: A Step-by-Step Guide*, *Vocabulary Improvement*, and *Easy English: Basic Grammar and Usage*.

Dedication and Acknowledgements

This book is dedicated to my husband, Gary Romero, who has shown me that being a good listener is easier than living with one.

Thank you, Carolyn Fierro, for your excellent work in formatting this text into the proper templates.

Thanks also to Donna Parker, who lent me her laptop for this adventure.

Preface

If you want to improve your ability to listen effectively in your business and personal life, this book is for you. Most of us aren't good listeners. While at work, normally we listen at about 25 percent of our ability. Most of us think we're good listeners and that overconfidence may be the reason for our downfall. Even if we devote full concentration to listening, we can't listen at 100 percent capacity for long. And at 100 percent, the message must be urgent to sustain our attention.

Aside from breathing, humans listen more than anything else we do. By reading and practicing the exercises in *The Business of Listening*, you'll learn to listen with more competence and skill. You'll improve if you have the desire, the interest, a high level of concentration, self-discipline, and a positive attitude.

This fourth edition provides you with improved listening know-how. Consider it the least you need to know to become a better listener. It provides helpful suggestions and exercises for improving your confidence and skills.

Use *The Business of Listening* as a reference, and challenge yourself to practice until you've mastered each new skill. Remember: Practice doesn't make perfect, it makes permanent.

Happy listening,

Diana Bonet Romero

Learning Objectives

Complete this book, and you'll know how to:

1) Discuss the benefits of listening—what's in it for you; what's in it for your organization.

2) Apply four key elements of good listening: hear, interpret, evaluate, and respond.

3) Identify your own listening style: promoting supportive, directive, or analytical.

4) Identify your own listening attitude.

5) Apply ten tips for tip-top listening.

Workplace and Management Competencies mapping

For over 30 years, business and industry has utilized competency models to select employees. The trend to use competency-based approaches in education and training, assessment, and development of workers has experienced a more recent emergence within the Employment and Training Administration (ETA), a division of the United States Department of Labor.

The ETA's General Competency Model Framework spans a wide array of competencies from the more basic competencies, such as reading and writing, to more advanced occupation-specific competencies. The Crisp Series finds its home in what the ETA refers to as the Workplace Competencies and the Management Competencies.

The Business of Listening covers information vital to mastering the following competencies:

Workplace Competencies:

▶ Customer Focus

Management Competencies:

▶ Supporting Others

For a comprehensive mapping of Crisp Series titles to the Workplace and Management competencies, visit www.CrispSeries.com.

About the Crisp 50-Minute Series

The Crisp 50-Minute Series was designed to cover critical business and professional development topics in the shortest possible time. Our easy-to-read, easy-to-understand format can be used for self-study or for classroom training. With a wealth of hands-on exercises, the 50-Minute books keep you engaged and help you retain critical skills.

What You Need to Know

We designed the Crisp 50-Minute Series to be as self-explanatory as possible. But there are a few things you should know before you begin the book.

Exercises

Exercises look like this:

EXERCISE TITLE

Questions and other information would be here.

Keep a pencil handy. Any time you see an exercise, you should try to complete it. If the exercise has specific answers, an answer key is provided in the appendix. (Some exercises ask you to think about your own opinions or situation; these types of exercises don't have answer keys.)

Forms

A heading like this means that the rest of the page is a form:

FORMHEAD

Forms are meant to be reusable. You might want to make a photocopy of a form before you fill it out, so that you can use it again later.

A Note to Instructors

We've tried to make the Crisp 50-Minute Series books as useful as possible as classroom training manuals. Here are some of the features we provide for instructors:

- ▶ PowerPoint presentations
- ▶ Answer keys
- ▶ Assessments
- ▶ Customization

PowerPoint Presentations

You can download a PowerPoint presentation for this book from our Web site at www.CrispSeries.com.

Answer keys

If an exercise has specific answers, an answer key will be provided in the appendix. (Some exercises ask you to think about your own opinions or situation; these types of exercises will not have answer keys.)

Assessments

For each 50-Minute Series book, we have developed a 35- to 50-item assessment. The assessment for this book is available at www.CrispSeries.com. *Assessments should not be used in any employee-selection process.*

Customization

Crisp books can be quickly and easily customized to meet your needs—from adding your logo to developing proprietary content. Crisp books are available in print and electronic form. For more information on customization, see www.CrispSeries.com.

6

P A R T 1

Why Should You Listen?

In this part:

▶ What's in It for You?

▶ What's in It for Your Organization?

▶ 50 Reasons to Become a Better Listener

▶ The Value of Small Changes

What's in It for You?

At least half of all communication time is spent listening. Experts in a dozen studies have concluded that we listen more than we perform any other activity, except breathing. Listening is the "receiving" part of communication. Listening is:

▶ Receiving information through your ears (and eyes)

▶ Giving meaning to (interpreting) that information

▶ Deciding what you think or feel about the information

▶ Responding to what you hear

Listening-related activities

Countless hours of listening are related to education and work. Following is a partial list of business-related activities that involve listening. Check (✓) each activity that applies to you.

❑ Attending meetings, briefings, or lectures

❑ Personal counseling (one-on-one)

❑ Receiving instructions

❑ Taking notes

❑ Interviewing others

❑ Making decisions based on verbal information

❑ Selling or marketing a product or service

❑ Managing others

❑ Servicing other groups or departments

❑ Answering telephones, cell phones, or beepers

If you're like most people, you checked many of the activities on this list. What other work-related activities can you think of that involve listening?

_____

_____

_____

_____

Why should you become a better listener? More important, what's in it for you? Put a check mark (✔) next to the items below with which you agree.

Listening effectively can:

- ❑ Increase your income
- ❑ Improve your company's profits
- ❑ Help you get promoted
- ❑ Increase your job satisfaction
- ❑ Improve your ability to solve problems
- ❑ Keep you aware of what's happening in your organization

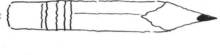

THE BENEFITS OF LISTENING

For each of the following statements, check **T** for true or **F** for false.

	T	F
1. Skill in listening improves your self-confidence.	❑	❑
2. People respect you more when you listen to them.	❑	❑
3. Good listeners usually complete their work.	❑	❑
4. Listening helps settle disagreements before they escalate.	❑	❑
5. Intelligent responses are easier when you listen.	❑	❑
6. Good listeners don't talk much.	❑	❑
7. Listening to clients helps you respond to them more quickly.	❑	❑
8. Few good listeners are promoted to top management positions.	❑	❑
9. Good listeners make fewer mistakes than poor listeners.	❑	❑
10. Handling distractions is difficult for good listeners.	❑	❑

Compare your answers to those of the author in the Appendix.

What's in It for Your Organization?

Successful organizations rely heavily upon listening as an important productivity tool. They seek to hire people who have good listening and communication skills. Employees who listen effectively help their employers by:

▶ Understanding problems

▶ Sustaining attention

▶ Retaining information

▶ Clarifying procedures

▶ Building relationships

Asleep at the Switch: The Cost of Lazy Listening

Most of us aren't good listeners. We listen at about 25 percent of our potential, which means we forget, ignore, distort, or misunderstand 75 percent of what we hear. That's hard to believe, perhaps, but true. Such lazy listening habits can be very costly, both to our business and to ourselves.

Poor listening is a significant problem in business today, because business relies on clear communication. When communication breaks down, costly mistakes occur. Organizations pay for these mistakes with lower profits, and consumers pay for the same mistakes with higher prices.

Lazy listening is a hidden cost of doing business. Suppose you were employed by a large international company with 10,000 employees. If each person in the company made a $100 error each year because of poor listening, the company would lose a million dollars. This loss would be especially bad news if your company had a profit-sharing plan or was forced to lay off workers because of low earnings.

The following case studies are true stories of the costs of lazy listening.

Three Case Studies

A sales manager for a large company asked his accounting department how he could charge off a $250,000 error caused by a dispatcher who routed a fleet of trucks to deliver building materials to the wrong state. The dispatcher heard the city (Portland), but not the state (Maine). The result was eight trucks 3,000 miles off course in Portland, Oregon. How could this problem have been avoided?

Three computer software representatives from different companies presented their products to a historical society that needed a special application. The historians dealt in rare manuscripts, and they were careful to explain to each representative what functions they required. Two of the representatives didn't listen effectively, so they presented inappropriate solutions. The third heard and understood what the historians wanted, and he got the order. The historians were impressed with only one thing. It wasn't the software, because they didn't know much about it yet. They did know that two people didn't listen and the third one did. They bought their programs from the one who listened. What was the cost to the other two companies?

Recently, Donna cut short a business trip to attend an important investment dinner meeting with her husband and their financial advisor. Donna hurried from the airport, dressed for dinner, and met her husband at the restaurant. An hour later, their financial advisor hadn't arrived. A cell phone call revealed that they were at the right restaurant but on the wrong night. The dinner was rescheduled, but Donna sacrificed profitable business she would have closed had she kept her original trip schedule. How can Donna avoid this problem in the future?

WHAT DO YOU KNOW ABOUT LISTENING?

Use this exercise to check your current awareness of this important personal skill. For each of the following statements, check **T** for true or **F** for false.

		T	F
1.	People who get the facts right are always good listeners.	☐	☐
2.	Listening involves more than your ears.	☐	☐
3.	Hearing isn't the same as listening.	☐	☐
4.	Good listening comes naturally when we pay attention.	☐	☐
5.	We can listen well and do other things at the same time.	☐	☐
6.	Posture affects listening.	☐	☐
7.	Most listening distractions can be controlled.	☐	☐
8.	If you can't remember something, you weren't really listening.	☐	☐
9.	Listening is a passive activity.	☐	☐
10.	Good listeners don't interrupt.	☐	☐

Compare your answers to those of the author in the Appendix.

50 Reasons to Become a Better Listener

Circle those that are most important to you.

1. To learn new skills
2. To be entertained
3. To understand a situation
4. To get information
5. To be respectful
6. To be responsible
7. To prevent accidents
8. To be a team player
9. To ask intelligent questions
10. To improve confidence
11. To protect freedom
12. To find out people's needs
13. To negotiate effectively
14. To be valued and trusted
15. To use money wisely
16. To be efficient and productive
17. To evaluate accurately
18. To compare logically
19. To share in your children's lives
20. To analyze a speaker's purpose
21. To be liked by others
22. To get the best value
23. To improve self-discipline
24. To build relationships
25. To solve problems
26. To show compassion
27. To satisfy curiosity
28. To be safe
29. To be an attentive lover
30. To make intelligent decisions
31. To prevent waste
32. To make money
33. To avoid embarrassment
34. To stay out of trouble
35. To save time and energy
36. To be an informed consumer
37. To be a supportive friend
38. To give an appropriate response
39. To enjoy the sounds of nature
40. To create win-win situations
41. To control distractions
42. To increase concentration ability
43. To improve vocabulary
44. To stay healthy
45. To prepare for shifts in conversations
46. To be a better family member
47. To settle disagreements
48. To maintain a flexible attitude
49. To improve your personality
50. To use the gift of listening

The Value of Small Changes

To improve the listening skills suggested in this book, we have to be both educated and motivated. We must believe that each positive small change in lazy listening habits has value.

Change can be hard work. Setbacks occur just when we think we're making progress. To change our bad listening habits, we must believe that the new skills we're gaining are worth more to us than the unproductive habits we're giving up. As you work to change your behavior and practice the listening techniques presented in the pages ahead, the following suggestions will be helpful.

1. **Notice small changes**. Recognize your improvements and give yourself a pat on the back. Acknowledging improvements is positive reinforcement.

2. **Keep a card** in your pocket to note significant listening habit changes, such as:

   ▷ Paid attention in a boring meeting.

   ▷ Received positive feedback from my manager about my communication skills.

   ▷ Stopped myself from interrupting a co-worker.

   ▷ Didn't allow distractions while talking on the phone.

   ▷ Made better eye contact while listening to staff members.

3. **Acknowledge setbacks** but don't give in to them. Failure to learn from mistakes is the only real failure.

4. **Stay with it.** Unless you work consciously to improve your listening skills, you'll find it easy to slip back into your old bad habits.

Part Summary

In this part, you learned what **better listening** can mean for **you**. Next, you learned what it can mean for **your organization**. You learned **50 reasons** for becoming a better listener. Finally, you learned that **change** can be hard work but is worth the effort.

Points to Remember

▶ Work and listening are inseparable.

▶ Lazy listening is a hidden cost in business.

▶ We listen for our own reasons.

▶ We can improve listening with desire, motivation, and a plan for constructive change.

Maybe we should have listened when he complained about the fluorescent lighting."

Four Key
Elements of
Good Listening

The greatest problem in communication is the illusion that it has been accomplished."

–Daniel W. Davenport

In this part:

- ▶ How to Be a Good Listener
- ▶ Key Element 1: Hear the Message
- ▶ Key Element 2: Interpret the Message
- ▶ Key Element 3: Evaluate the Message
- ▶ Key Element 4: Respond to the Message
- ▶ Review

How to Be a Good Listener

Good listening is an active, integrated communication skill that demands energy and know-how. It's purposeful, powerful, and productive. To listen effectively, we must hear and select information from the speaker, give it meaning, determine how we feel about it, and respond—in a matter of seconds.

Also, we must understand the speaker's purpose, which influences the way we listen and how we perceive the message. The speaker and the listener must have the same purpose, if communication is to be effective. Next time you listen to someone, make sure you're aware of the speaker's purpose.

Is he or she:

- ❑ Entertaining you?
- ❑ Instructing you?
- ❑ Providing critical data?
- ❑ Persuading you?
- ❑ Sharing feelings?
- ❑ Making small talk?

For example, if Larry is making small talk, you can enjoy the conversation for its own sake. You and Larry are building rapport and strengthening your relationship with this casual conversation. However, if you and Larry are in a meeting and he's informing you of important business procedures, you'll be listening for facts, numbers, and other key information. Probably you'll be taking notes and asking questions to clarify the information.

Four Key Elements

The four key elements of the listening process describe what good listeners do to listen well in any situation. No matter what listening situation you're in, the following four elements apply:

1. Hear the message
2. Interpret the message
3. Evaluate the message
4. Respond to the message

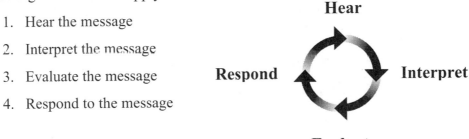

ARE YOU A GOOD LISTENER?

Before reading the four elements of good listening, consider what you already know about yourself as a listener. Remember that we listen differently at different times to different people.

Evaluate yourself at the beginning of this section, then put a check-in date on your calendar two weeks from today. Return to this page and reevaluate to see if any of your numbers change. They'll change positively if you commit to doing something about negative listening habits. It's up to you.

Following are 10 characteristics of a good listener. On a scale of 1-5, with 5 being the highest, fill in the blanks to indicate the degree to which you already practice these positive listening behaviors.

Go through the list twice, first rating yourself with the person you listen to the best, then with the person to whom you find it the most difficult to listen.

	Best	Worst	
1.	___	___	I make appropriate eye contact with the speaker.
2.	___	___	I ask questions for clarification.
3.	___	___	I show concern by acknowledging feelings.
4.	___	___	I restate or paraphrase some of the speaker's words to show that I understand.
5.	___	___	I seek first to understand, then to be understood.
6.	___	___	I'm poised and emotionally controlled.
7.	___	___	I react nonverbally, with a smile, a nod, a frown, or a touch (if appropriate).
8.	___	___	I pay close attention and don't let my mind wander.
9.	___	___	I react responsibly to what I hear.
10.	___	___	I stick to the subject.

IDENTIFYING BAD LISTENING HABITS

Following is a list of 10 bad habits of listening. On a scale of 1-5, with 5 being the worst case, indicate the degree to which you're guilty of these faux pas.

Rate yourself twice, first with the person you listen to best, then with the person to whom you find it most difficult to listen. Be honest with yourself. Recognizing how you listen is the first step toward beneficial change.

Best **Worst**

1. ___ ___ I interrupt often.

2. ___ ___ I jump to conclusions.

3. ___ ___ I finish their sentences.

4. ___ ___ I change the subject without warning.

5. ___ ___ I would rather talk than listen.

6. ___ ___ I pay attention only halfway.

7. ___ ___ I don't give any verbal or nonverbal indication that I've heard what was said.

8. ___ ___ I'm an impatient listener.

9. ___ ___ I become defensive quickly.

10. ___ ___ I think about my reply while he or she is speaking.

Key Element 1: Hear the Message

Hearing is the beginning of the listening process. You might hear a door slam, a truck driving by, or a familiar voice. The brain recognizes sound as it enters the ear. Then the other "listening channels," such as our eyes and our emotions, kick in. All channels seek consistency or inconsistency and confirmation of the spoken message from the speaker's nonverbal feedback, such as body language and tone of voice.

Hearing itself is non-selective and involuntary, such as hearing the sound of a siren. However, when you choose to listen, it's on purpose.

Listening Is Voluntary

From the constant noise around us, we select what we want to recognize. This information moves from short-term memory (STM) to long-term memory (LTM). STM is a "holding pen" for signals from our senses. To protect us from overstimulation, STM has limited capacity and is easily disrupted. For example, a clerk wouldn't likely retain much from a technical discussion about data transport protocols, because he or she has no use for the information. The information would probably be held in STM for 1 to 30 seconds. If information isn't recognized and isn't selected for processing into LTM, it's dismissed from STM and then forgotten.

In a sense, we're preprogrammed. Our choice of what to listen to comes from our past choices. Previous choices are based on interests and needs. John likes to invest in the stock market, so he always has his "ears open" for tips on hot stocks. Ellie "tunes in" whenever someone is discussing consumer rights. Julio "catches" the football scores each Sunday to track his favorite teams. In other words, we choose what we want to listen to, and often it's based on our past choices.

In order to listen to someone, we begin by hearing and selecting their oral messages and taking in the accompanying nonverbal signals. When these messages are interesting or important, we pay attention.

We choose to listen because:

▶ The message is important or urgent.

▶ We're interested in the information.

▶ We care about the subject or the person speaking.

▶ We feel like listening.

▶ We have time to listen.

▶ We listened to this kind of information in the past.

▶ We like/respect the person speaking.

▶ We want to be liked and to make a good impression.

Sometimes, even when we choose to listen, anger, frustration, grief, or fatigue can act as emotional earplugs. We tend to hear what we expect or want to hear, and we filter out that which isn't consistent with our expectations.

Jennifer was on her way to lunch when her manager dropped a report on her desk and said he needed 20 sets of copies when he returned from lunch. Jennifer was upset, because her friends were waiting and she assumed she had to make the copies immediately. She didn't hear her boss say after *his* lunch, which was an hour later than hers. If she'd listened carefully, she would have had ample time to make the copies after she returned from her lunch.

Five Keys to Hearing the Message

▶ Care.

▶ Pay attention.

▶ Focus on what's important.

▶ Be willing to listen to new information.

▶ Factor in your emotional filters.

"Gosh, how embarrassing."

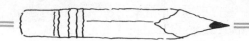

LISTENING LAB 1: HEARING THE MESSAGE

Sit quietly someplace where people are talking around you: your cubicle, hotel lobby, office corridor, airport. Listen for about 10 minutes, then write down what you heard (i.e., what people said and other incidental sounds and noises.)

This activity should make you conscious of the many voices and sounds that bombard us daily. It reminds you that listening begins with hearing, remembering that hearing is a voluntary activity.

1. What did you hear? _____

_____

_____

2. How many sounds do you remember? _____

3. What sounds did you remember most easily? _____

_____

_____

4. Did your mind wander while you were listening? _____

5. Try the experiment again with your eyes closed and see if the results are the same. (You'll notice how important your eyes are to listening.)

_____

_____

_____

Compare your answers to those of the author in the Appendix.

LISTENING LAB 2: HEARING THE MESSAGE

Listed below are some methods for improving listening at the hearing level. Write any others you can think of. Select one specific method to work on for the next three days. At the end of the three days, assign yourself a number grade between one and five, with five as the highest.

▶ Improve your vocabulary so that words and meanings are clear when you listen.

▶ Have your hearing checked. (See author's note below.)

▶ Ask for repetition or clarification.

▶ Overcome any tendency to daydream.

▶ Eliminate distractions.

Others:

_____

_____

_____

Author's Note What irony! Several years ago, I was talking on the phone, and the speaker's voice sounded garbled and far away. When I switched ears, everything was fine. I had a hearing test, followed by an MRI. The diagnosis was an acoustic neuroma, a growth on the hearing nerve in my left ear. I had surgery, and it was removed, but it had killed the hearing nerve. I can hear just fine out of my right ear, but the event was life-changing. Acoustic neuromas are uncommon, but if you even suspect that you're having trouble hearing, please have your hearing checked.

Key Element 2: Interpret the Message

Interpreting a speaker's message means coming to a mutual understanding of the speaker's meaning. Good listeners know that a match-up in meaning is a match-up in understanding. The word, *communication*, comes from the Latin root word *communis,* which means "commonness," a commonness of understanding.

Often, listeners experience problems at the interpreting level, because no two people perceive information in the same way. Speakers don't always say exactly what they mean—or mean exactly what they say.

What's the difference?

"When I look at you, time stands still."

"You have a face that would stop a clock."

It's unlikely that we interpret accurately in most listening situations. Listening is a complicated process. Speakers send messages to listeners both verbally and nonverbally. If Jim tells Lavon, "You have to do something about the Doughty account," Lavon must assign meaning to Jim's words, mental filters, tone of voice, and the nonverbal cues. It's at the interpreting level that Lavon seeks to understand Jim's meaning in the way that Jim intended it.

Following are four important elements to consider when seeking to interpret another's meaning.

Words

Here's something interesting. Words themselves have little meaning. Words are merely vehicles for the thoughts and feelings of the speaker. Words aren't the same as experiences; they're a means of explaining experiences. Have you ever said, "I can't tell you how happy I am"? You feel the happiness and excitement, but the word, *happy*, is much less than the emotion you feel. It's the people speaking who give meaning to the words, rather than the words giving meaning to the people who speak them.

Filters

Both listeners and speakers have mental filters that help or hinder the interpreting process. These filters are in our brain's personal database, and they attach our own meaning to the information we receive. Therefore, be aware of your filters, so that you control your own perceptions while listening. Some examples of our personal filters include the following. Can you add others?

memories	attitudes
assumptions	biases, such as political affiliation or religion
expectations	emotional hot-buttons
current attention span	past experiences
values	knowledge and intelligence
feelings	self-esteem
language and vocabulary	needs and motives
age	sensory acuity

Tone of Voice

Voice conveys approximately 30 percent of the meaning of a message. Voices can be calm, strident, pleading, questioning, whiney, etc. Think of tone as the mood of someone's voice. When people end their sentences on an upward note, they sound like questions; the speakers sound as if they're asking permission to speak. Also, they sound uncertain about their convictions. To change this perception, speakers should let their voices drop slightly at the end of each sentence.

Try this: Say the following sentence twice—first with a question at the end, then dropping your voice at the end. Which one sounds more self-assured?

I'm leaving the office at 5:00?

I'm leaving the office at 5:00.

Tom speaks in a quiet monotone. Even though he's intelligent, his voice lacks conviction, and people don't take him seriously. What could Tom do with his voice to get people to listen to him?

There's an old saying, "Fake it 'til you make it." Try sounding sure of yourself and authoritative by dropping your voice consciously at the end of each sentence. Also avoid the word, *like*. You'll sound "like" really grown up. Probably you'll surprise yourself.

Tone of voice tells the listener a great deal about the speaker. And the better we know someone, the more we depend on tone to tell us what he or she really means.

Nonverbal Cues

A nonverbal cue, or body language, is a message sent by a speaker's gestures, facial expressions, posture, and eyes. Good listeners interpret a speaker's nonverbal feedback through five sensory channels: ears, eyes, heart, mind, and intuition. Nonverbal cues, along with tone of voice, confirm or deny the message of the words. More than half of most human interaction is through nonverbal communication.

▶ Who's easier to approach, someone who's smiling or someone who's frowning?

▶ Who seems more confident, someone with poor posture or someone who stands up straight?

▶ Whom do you trust more, someone who makes no eye contact or someone who looks you in the eye?

Three Keys to Interpreting the Message

▶ Understand your filters.

▶ Listen to the tone of a message.

▶ Read nonverbal signals.

> *Good listeners want to understand the speaker's meaning. They're aware of their own filters and those of the speaker, and they ask questions when they want clarification."*
>
> **–Anonymous**

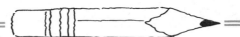

LISTENING LAB 3: INTERPRETING THE MESSAGE

Imagine that you've just interviewed a young woman for an important position in your department. As she's leaving, she remembers one last thing and states, "By the way, I graduated in the top 10 percent of my class." Then she shakes your hand, thanks you for the interview, and leaves.

Following are some interpretations of her statement. Read these, then list other possible interpretations.

1. She's intelligent.

2. She's competitive.

3. The school wasn't academically challenging.

4. She studied constantly.

5. She brags a lot.

6. _____

7. _____

How would you clarify your interpretation?

_____

_____

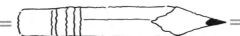

LISTENING LAB 4: INTERPRETING THE MESSAGE

Say the following sentence out loud seven times.

"I never said you stole the money."

Each time you say it, emphasize a different word. For example, the first time through, emphasize the word *"I." I* never said you stole the money.

This example shows how voice emphasis influences the interpretation of information. To become a better communicator, listen carefully to the speaker's voice inflection and word emphasis. Ask what the speaker means if you aren't sure.

Key Element 3: Evaluate the Message

Good listeners make sure they have all of the key information before forming an opinion. They don't jump to conclusions based on a bias or incomplete information. They may agree with the speaker, or they may disagree. Good listening doesn't mean automatic compliance. A good listener weighs and analyzes all of the evidence before reaching a decision or making a judgment.

Gayle is a member of a jury trying a felony case. As each attorney sifts through the evidence, Gayle listens carefully for validation as she forms her opinions. She recognizes her personal biases but seeks to remain objective. She's careful not to jump to conclusions based on emotional testimony. At the end of the trial, Gayle evaluates all of the evidence presented by both sides before stating her decision. The jury foreman later thanks Gayle for her valuable observations and objective comments.

We make conscientious evaluations when we make decisions based on all the available information. We run into problems with evaluation when we think mechanically or jump to conclusions. We must ask ourselves if we're listening to or listening against that person. Are we evaluating or making a value judgment?

Evaluation isn't required in every situation (listening to music, hearing an entertaining story); therefore, we also must know our purpose for listening.

Three Keys to Evaluate the Message

▶ Ask questions.

▶ Analyze all the evidence.

▶ Don't jump to conclusions.

LISTENING LAB 5: EVALUATING THE MESSAGE

We listen to constant advertising and opinions in the media. The Internet provides a barrage of information—some of it questionable, some reliable. How often do you stop to evaluate the slant or bias of advertisers who want you to buy products or try services? How often do you ask if the information is reasonable and logical? Do you ask yourself what they *aren't* telling you?

Following is a description of Adolph Hitler, as it may have been written by his publicist. Read the description as if you were listening to it, taking note of the writer's built-in bias. Then answer the questions that follow.

> Solely through his own efforts, our leader overcame an unhappy childhood in which he received little formal education. His father bitterly opposed his ambition to become an artist. Through self-education, he became the author of a national bestseller while jailed as a political prisoner. Obstacles don't discourage him. When others say, "It's impossible," he hurdles each barrier as it comes.
>
> He has built an active youth movement of selected young people. He's known throughout the world for his dynamic speeches and seeks to change relationships with neighboring countries. Close associates say of him, "He accomplishes incredible deeds out of the passion of his will in order to create the kind of government he believes in."

1. How would you evaluate Hitler if you hadn't heard of him before you read this description?

   _____

2. Are any character flaws suggested in the description?

   _____

3. What methods does the publicist use to create a positive impression?

   _____

   _____

4. How will this exercise help you evaluate information more carefully?

   _____

Key Element 4: Respond to the Message

Although a response may be considered a speaking rather than a listening role, it's still critical to clear communication. The listener must let the speaker know, by verbal and/or nonverbal feedback, what was heard and how it was heard.

Good listeners accept responsibility to provide feedback for the speaker to complete the communication process. Good listeners have a strong desire to reach a common understanding.

Responsible responses inform the speaker that:

> ▶ The message was heard.
>
> ▶ It was understood.
>
> ▶ It was evaluated appropriately.

Several problems can occur here. One problem is when no response occurs. If Karla asks Jack when the plans for the office remodel will be available, and Jack simply stares at Karla without indicating that he heard her, he isn't communicating effectively. Although silence can communicate to a degree, a blank stare isn't a helpful response.

Other problems include responses that are defensive, overly emotional, or otherwise inappropriate. If Jack had changed the subject abruptly, his response would have been inappropriate. Finally, a confusing response (i.e., a double message) can occur when verbal and nonverbal feedback are in conflict.

If Jack had smiled in a friendly manner, but his voice sounded hostile as he replied, "Why do you want to know?" he would have confused Karla. He was sending two messages—one with his voice and one with his smile. Double messages are difficult to decode. Often, they're used by someone who's afraid of the consequences of telling the truth.

Three Keys to Responding to the Message

> ▶ Seek a common understanding.
>
> ▶ Acknowledge what you hear.
>
> ▶ Avoid double messages.

LISTENING LAB 6: RESPONDING TO THE MESSAGE

Following are several possible responses in listening situations. Place a check mark (✓) next to those you think are important for good communication.

_____ 1. Providing prompt feedback

_____ 2. Giving feedback that's relevant to the conversation

_____ 3. Changing the subject

_____ 4. Checking your cell phone messages

_____ 5. Using appropriate eye contact

_____ 6. Matching verbal and nonverbal feedback for consistency

_____ 7. Staring blankly

_____ 8. Asking a question for clarification

_____ 9. Mumbling

_____ 10. Interpreting

_____ 11. Paraphrasing some of what the speaker said

_____ 12. Responding defensively

Add your own responses below:

_____

_____

Review Lab for Key Elements 1-4

Review each of the key elements in the listening process: hear, interpret, evaluate and respond. Then meet a co-worker for coffee and observe yourself going through the four steps when it's your turn to listen.

The following checklist focuses on each key element and evaluates your awareness of your listening behavior. Put a check (✓) next to each answer that applies.

Review Lab for Key Element 1: Hearing the Message

During our conversation, did I:

❑ Care about my co-worker's attitudes, opinions, and beliefs?

❑ Pay close attention?

❑ Ask for clarification when I didn't understand something?

❑ Allow myself to become distracted?

❑ Seek to understand the feelings behind the words?

❑ Listen carefully enough to remember what my co-worker said?

List here three specific points made by my co-worker:

_____

_____

_____

Review Lab for Key Element 2: Interpreting the Message

During our conversation, did I:

❑ Notice any words that were used in an unusual context?

❑ Ask questions for clarification?

❑ Pay attention to his or her tone of voice?

❑ Watch for nonverbal cues, such as facial expressions or gestures?

❑ Notice if body language, tone, and words all conveyed the same message?

❑ Let my own filters interfere with my co-worker's meaning?

Two questions I asked to make sure that I understood my co-worker's meaning:

_____

_____

Review Lab for Key Element 3: Evaluating the Message

During our conversation, did I

- ❑ Believe everything I heard?
- ❑ Agree with everything I heard?
- ❑ Disagree agreeably?
- ❑ Weigh and analyze all of the information before responding?
- ❑ Jump to conclusions?
- ❑ Ask questions when I needed more information?
- ❑ Evaluate the information rather than judge the person?

I evaluated two of my co-worker's statements as follows:

_____

_____

Review Lab for Key Element 4: Responding to the Message

During our conversation, did I:

- ❑ Take responsibility for my responses?
- ❑ Look and act interested?
- ❑ Repeat information for clarity?
- ❑ Rush the speaker?
- ❑ Match my verbal and nonverbal responses?

I took responsibility for my responses in the following ways:

_____

_____

Part Summary

In this part, you learned how to be a **good listener**. You learned how to use the four key elements of good listening: **hear** the message, **interpret** the message, **evaluate** the message, and **respond** to the message.

Points to Remember

▶ Hear the message. Listen to and notice both verbal and nonverbal information.

▶ Interpret the message. The best interpretation is a match-up of meaning between the speaker and the listener.

▶ Evaluate the message. The listener's opinion should be based on all available information. Ask questions.

▶ Respond to the message. Good listening means giving the speaker an appropriate response, verbally and/or nonverbally.

Your Listening

Style

> " *I know that you believe you understand what you think I said, but I am not sure you realize that what you heard is not what I meant.*"
>
> **–Anonymous**

In this part:

- ▶ You are Unique
- ▶ The Promoting Style
- ▶ The Supporting Style
- ▶ The Directive Style
- ▶ The Analytical Style

You Are Unique

Each of us has a personal view of how the world should turn. Your personal values, upbringing, beliefs, attitudes, and behaviors combine to make up your unique style. In this section, four different styles of listening are examined. They are:

▶ The Promoting Style

▶ The Supporting Style

▶ The Directive Style

▶ The Analytical Style

Following are descriptions of these styles that could apply to how you perceive information, communicate, and act. Naturally, your style influences the way you listen. When you've read the descriptions, decide which of the four styles comes closest to your preferred means of listening and communicating in general.

Note: No one uses just one style. We're combinations of all styles, but you'll probably see yourself more in one style than in the others. Often, we see other people's styles (those of co-workers, family, friends) before we recognize our own.

Don't get locked in here. This information has real value in helping you to understand more clearly your needs and expectations as a listener. But take it with a grain of salt.

"My ears just fell off! Hold my calls!"

The Promoting Style

The Good Stuff

These folks are peppy! They have lots of energy, and they get excited about things. Their positive, outgoing natures motivate everyone. As team members, promoters see the big picture. They're inventive, confident, and idealistic about reaching goals. In meetings, they keep things stirred up by cracking jokes and injecting ideas (even when they aren't asked). The promoting style is sociable and fun to be around.

The Downside

Promoters are always on the leading edge with new ideas, but they aren't good at following through. They prefer to leave the grunt work to someone who enjoys that sort of thing. They tend to overpromise, which causes them to be late a lot. A promoter's screensaver might read: "Deadlines amuse me."

Some people see promoters as superficial, because they move quickly from one idea to another without following through. As a result, they seem to be disorganized.

Tips for Better Listening

If you have a promoting style, you have a strong personality. Toning down your style and forcefulness can make you less intimidating to others. You don't do well at tolerating indirect communication, so be patient (this is important), and ask questions to understand other people's meanings.

Because of your attention-getting style, you'll have trouble giving up your preoccupation with yourself. To be a good listener, seek first to understand, then seek to be understood.

Some people perceive your bubbly enthusiasm as insincere and too much pie in the sky. Balance your energetic style with common sense, and be realistic about keeping promises. If you say you'll meet a deadline, do it. You don't have to give up your style in order to be a good listener, but if you match your style to that of the speaker, you'll communicate more effectively.

How to Get a Promoter's Attention

If you want promoters to listen to you, speak forcefully and clearly, use big gestures, paint visual pictures, and lose the detail! You won't hold their attention for long, so plan what you say and use humor (if you're funny). Include small talk and don't back away from conflict. (Promoters usually enjoy it.) It's easier to get their attention if you meet with them in a private conference room and their Blackberries are out of reach.

PROMOTER'S LISTENING STYLE

If you see yourself as having a promoting style, answer the following questions:

1. Why do you identify yourself as having a promoting style?

_____

_____

2. Based on your style, what are your current strengths as a listener?

_____

_____

3. Based on your style, what are your current weaknesses as a listener?

_____

_____

4. What do you like people to do or say to show that they're listening to you?

_____

_____

5. Given the information about your style, how do you plan to improve your listening? List three behaviors.

_____

_____

_____

The Supporting Style

The Good Stuff

These folks give new meaning to the word *nice*. Their friendly, helpful style makes them the ultimate team players. They're easy-going and spontaneous, and they take things as they come. They prefer to work in groups and make decisions by consensus. Their decisions are based on the effects their actions will have on others.

In meetings, the supporting style is a peacemaker who seeks to make co-workers comfortable and happy. And they usually bring cookies. Their screensavers might say, "How may I help you?"

The Downside

Because of their need for acceptance, people with supporting style don't always say what they think. They vacillate in order to please people. They don't do well at setting personal goals. They'd rather help other people reach **their** goals. This style operates more on feelings than facts, and they fight with feelings as well.

People with more forceful styles see those with supporting style as easy marks, because they can't say no. People with this style also tend to waste time, because they're very social, and they don't take initiative to get things done.

Tips for Better Listening

As a supporter, you do a lot of listening. However, you're more tuned to feelings than to facts. Therefore, you must listen carefully when facts are involved—which is most of the time in a business environment. Take notes and ask questions for clarification. Be sure to provide feedback on what you hear, then act quickly and responsibly to fulfill your commitments.

Learn to say no—a legitimate response at times. Set limits with people on the amount of time you spend listening, especially if you have work to do—for example, "I can spend five minutes with you, then I need to finish filling this order."

Learn to be assertive and to face dominant personalities without backing down. Listen to them, paraphrase, then state your opinion clearly and directly. These actions on your part will gain their respect.

How to Get a Supporter's Attention

This one is easy. Supporters are natural listeners, because they want to please. If your style is more forceful (most styles are), tone it down and speak quietly and casually. Take time to engage in small talk and be willing to add a personal touch to your discussion. Compliments about their work are appropriate.

The supporting style tends to listen more for feelings than facts, so include feelings with facts, such as, "I'd sure feel good about having this report on my desk by three o'clock." Be specific about facts—especially deadlines—because time gets away from supporters very quickly.

Ask for confirmation of information to be sure a supporter heard you correctly. It doesn't hurt to check in on a supporter's progress on a project. Supporters enjoy the attention, and it keeps them on track.

Quietly praise their work with gentle, "feeling" words. "I liked the way you handled that call." The supporting style doesn't adapt easily to change, so give plenty of warning when changes will occur.

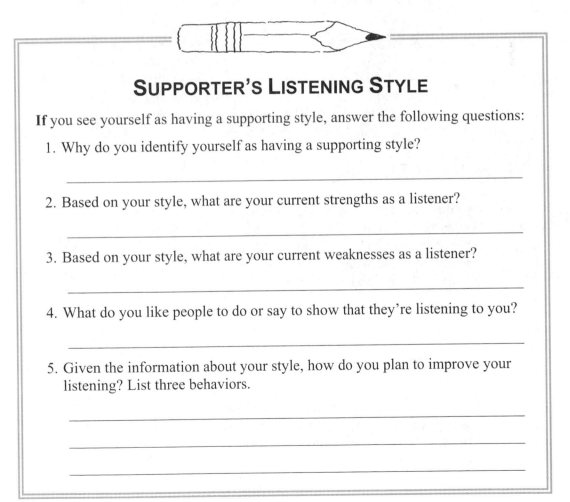

SUPPORTER'S LISTENING STYLE

If you see yourself as having a supporting style, answer the following questions:

1. Why do you identify yourself as having a supporting style?

   _____

2. Based on your style, what are your current strengths as a listener?

   _____

3. Based on your style, what are your current weaknesses as a listener?

   _____

4. What do you like people to do or say to show that they're listening to you?

   _____

5. Given the information about your style, how do you plan to improve your listening? List three behaviors.

   _____

   _____

   _____

The Directive Style

The Good Stuff

Like a human bulldozer, the person with directive style plows through obstacles, ignores excuses, and gets things done. The person with this non-emotional, take-charge style approaches problems boldly and realistically.

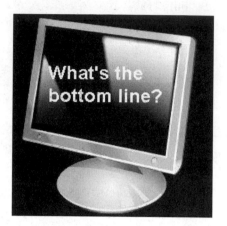

Such people dominate and control because of their forceful natures. With a director, winning is everything. These hard chargers don't waste time or money, and they're realistic about both. When situations get tough, they tighten the controls. They value achievement and expect big rewards (yachts, money, islands). Their screensavers might read, "What's the bottom line?"

The Downside

Directors aren't known for humility. They have big egos, and they play to win. They seldom praise or give credit to others. Sometimes, they're downright critical and insensitive. They expect a lot, and they're ornery and demanding when they don't get results. Generally, they aren't good listeners.

Tips for Better Listening

If you have a directive style, you're a good listener who doesn't listen. Patience. Patience. Patience. This commodity is in short supply in Director Land, so make it a priority. Develop enough humility to admit that lots of folks have good ideas but that your forceful style intimidates them. You use intimidation, because you don't want to be used by those who have your ear.

Lighten up and set aside more time for your co-workers, family, and friends. Try style flexing to become more approachable. (Style flexing is an effort to follow another's style by modeling that person's behavior, such as, lowering your voice, if the other speaks softly, approximating another's body language, using some of the same words used by the person to whom you're listening.)

When you hear a good idea, give credit, even praise. You don't suffer fools lightly, but people with good ideas don't always express themselves well. Again, patience. Ask for feedback; ask for advice from time to time. Did we mention patience?

How to Get a Director's Attention

First, make an appointment and plan what you'll say. Organize your ideas. They'll give you five minutes; you give them the bottom line. Anticipate questions and be prepared with sensible persuasive answers.

Deal in accurate facts and figures. Don't beat around the bush. (You won't have time for that anyway.) Support your arguments and point of view with logic and realistic data. Forget small talk unless he or she initiates it, but keep it to a minimum. When people with directive styles listen to you and like what you have to say, they're likely to act quickly and boldly to implement your ideas (for which they also may take the credit).

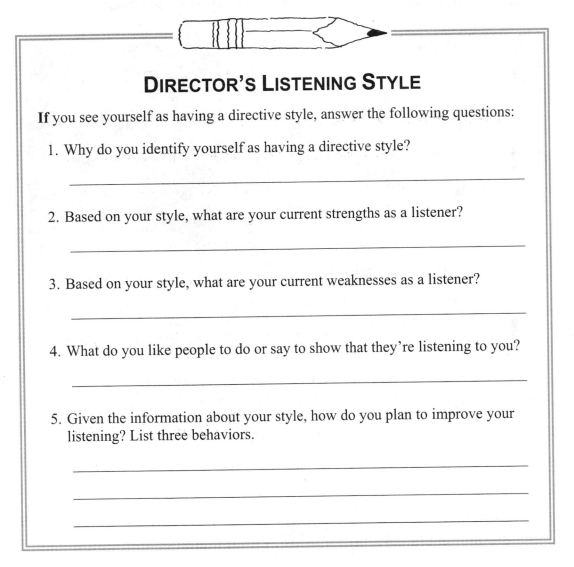

DIRECTOR'S LISTENING STYLE

If you see yourself as having a directive style, answer the following questions:

1. Why do you identify yourself as having a directive style?

   _____

2. Based on your style, what are your current strengths as a listener?

   _____

3. Based on your style, what are your current weaknesses as a listener?

   _____

4. What do you like people to do or say to show that they're listening to you?

   _____

5. Given the information about your style, how do you plan to improve your listening? List three behaviors.

   _____

   _____

   _____

The Analytical Style

The Good Stuff

This style is, above all, logical. Analytical types are usually neat, organized, and precise. Therefore, they lean toward professions that require these qualities—engineering, science, accounting, research, and the like. As excellent problem-solvers, they contribute to their work teams with a thorough knowledge of the subject, an objective analysis of available information, and a practical game plan.

They prefer to spend their time with other experienced, knowledgeable people. They keep agreements and meet deadlines on time. They're dependable and patient.

The Downside

With so many positive qualities, it's hard to imagine a downside. That depends on whom you ask. Some would say that rightness can turn quickly to self-righteousness, and insistence on complete accuracy soon becomes tedious and boring. Stubbornness becomes an art form, and the push for perfection makes analyzers ever so picky about the smallest details. Their screensavers might read, "I'm right! I'm right! I'm right!"

Tips for Better Listening

Your security is in being right. If you don't get this confirmation, you soon tune out. Resist the temptation, and keep listening. Learn to accept other people's ideas as valid. Find the logic and truth in their points of view. Develop a sense of humor. The world is a pretty funny place.

You aren't much of a risk-taker, so open your mind to new ideas and be willing to stretch your imagination. Your fear of being wrong makes you stubbornly resistant to listening to information that contradicts your point of view. There's more than one way to peel a potato, so listen louder. As they say, even a broken clock is right twice a day.

How to Get an Analyzer's Attention

Rule one: Make sense. Be logical and organized in your presentation, and be prepared to support your data with facts – lots of them. Keep small talk to a minimum, as analyzers are quite internal people who consider small talk a waste of time. And they aren't very good at small talk themselves. Sprinkle your conversations with phrases like, "You're right about that," and "You sure figured that one out in a hurry." "I hadn't thought of that," works too, because you probably hadn't. If people with analytical styles don't respond to your questions right away, they're thinking, so give them the time they need. They'll reward you with a reasonable well-thought-out answer.

ANALYZER'S LISTENING STYLE

If you see yourself as having an analytical style, answer the following questions:

1. Why do you identify yourself as having an analytical style?

   _____

2. Based on your style, what are your current strengths as a listener?

   _____

3. Based on your style, what are your current weaknesses as a listener?

   _____

4. What do you like people to do or say to show that they're listening to you?

   _____

5. Given the information about your style, how do you plan to improve your listening? List three behaviors.

   _____

   _____

   _____

OPTIONAL PRACTICE

With a friend, a co-worker, or a small group, discuss the various communication styles. Determine your styles and discuss how they're the same and how they differ from one another.

If your styles are the same, discuss how they're alike and how you can listen effectively to those whose styles are different.

If your styles are different, discuss how you like to be approached in a conversation and how you like to be listened to.

Don't (do, say, act like) this if you want me to listen.

_____

_____

Please (do, say act like) this if you want me to listen.

_____

_____

Discuss what each of you can do to become a better listener.

Part Summary

In this part, you learned that each of us is **unique** and has his or her own style. You learned how to recognize each of the four **listening styles**, one of which you probably use more than others. You learned that the listening styles include the **Promoting** Style, the **Supporting** Style, the **Directive** Style, and the **Analytical** Style.

Points to Remember

▶ Everyone is different.

▶ Those with promoting styles listen for the big picture.

▶ Those with supporting styles listen for feelings.

▶ Those with directive styles listen for the bottom line.

▶ Those with analytical styles listen for facts.

What Is Your
Listening Attitude?

" *The greatest compliment that was ever paid me was when someone asked what I thought, and attended to my answer.*"

—Henry David Thoreau

In this part:

- ▶ A Listening Attitude: Your Key to Success
- ▶ Barriers to Communication
- ▶ Bridges to Communication
- ▶ How Well Do You Listen?
- ▶ How to Stop Bad Listening Habits
- ▶ How to Help Someone Listen to You

A Listening Attitude: Your Key to Success

What kind of a listener are you? Bored? Conscientious? Distracted? Thoughtful? This section provides you with some self-evaluation tools. What's your listening attitude? How well does it contribute to your overall success in business? In school? In your personal life?

Most of us believe that we're good listeners. As previously noted, however, research indicates that, on average, we're effective listeners at an efficiency level of only 25 percent. Much of the time, we **think** we're listening. We seem to believe that, because we have ears, we're listening. This is like believing that, because we have eyes, we can read.

Unconscious attitudes and undiagnosed bad habits—such as interrupting, allowing ourselves to become distracted, jumping to conclusions, daydreaming, or giving in to boredom—prevent us from becoming the kinds of listeners we think we are. The only way to improve is to make conscious choices to change.

If you want to be effective, plan positive action steps, then practice specific listening skills at every opportunity. These steps will improve your ability to listen. The exercises in this section will help you evaluate your listening attitudes and resulting behaviors so that you can plan your strategy.

LISTENING LAB: WHAT'S YOUR LISTENING ATTITUDE?

Developing listening skills is an ongoing process, and discovering your attitude about listening is an important first step. To discover your listening attitudes, complete this exercise. Check Yes (Y) or No (N) for each statement.

	Y	N
1. I stop what I'm doing in order to listen.	❏	❏
2. I listen carefully for main ideas and supporting points.	❏	❏
3. I take notes during meetings to help me remember key points.	❏	❏
4. I ignore most distractions.	❏	❏
5. I keep my emotions under control.	❏	❏
6. I disagree agreeably.	❏	❏
7. I wait for the speaker to finish before evaluating the message.	❏	❏
8. I respond appropriately with a smile or an acknowledgment.	❏	❏
9. I'm aware of mannerisms that may distract a speaker and keep mine under control.	❏	❏
10. I know my biases and control them when I'm listening.	❏	❏
11. I refrain from interrupting.	❏	❏
12. I value eye contact and maintain it most of the time.	❏	❏
13. I restate or paraphrase to be sure I have the correct meaning.	❏	❏
14. I listen for emotional meaning in addition to content.	❏	❏
15. I ask questions for clarification.	❏	❏
16. I respect others' opinions, even when I disagree.	❏	❏
17. When listening on the phone, I keep a hand free to take notes.	❏	❏
18. I attempt to set aside my ego and focus on the speaker.	❏	❏
19. I'm careful to judge the message rather than the messenger.	❏	❏
20. I'm a patient listener most of the time.	❏	❏

CONTINUED

CONTINUED

Scoring

The following scale will help you interpret your present listening skill level based on your current attitudes and behaviors. How many "No" answers did you accumulate?

  1 to 5:   You're an excellent listener. Keep it up!

  6 to 10: You're a good listener, but you can improve.

11 to 15: Through practice ,you can become a much better listener.

16 to 20: Listen up!

"I said I'm taking a course in the power of speech."

Barriers to Communication

Our attitudes about certain people or particular subjects greatly affect our listening behavior. Attitudes can be a bridge or a barrier to good communication. Listeners can avoid the barriers to listening by understanding the pitfalls and knowing how to avoid them.

Following are descriptions of some listening attitudes. Answer the questions following each description in order to help these characters improve their listening behaviors.

VACANT VINCENT

The most difficult person to communicate with is a daydreamer. Meet Vacant Vincent. You'll recognize him by the faraway look in his eye. Vincent is a social butterfly who dips in and out of conversations, picking up bits and pieces of information. He's physically present but not really there. Vincent is easily distracted and often changes the subject without warning. Sometimes he slouches, plays with his tie, or answers text messages. The best way to get Vincent's attention is to talk about his interests.

What's Vincent's attitude?

_____

How can Vincent become a better listener? Following is a list of possible behaviors. Put a check mark next to any that would help Vincent to improve his communication skills.

❏ 1. Sitting in a listening position   ❏ 5. Making eye contact

❏ 2. Controlling distractions   ❏ 6. Sticking to the subject

❏ 3. Chewing his nails   ❏ 7. Mental channel-surfing

❏ 4. Taking an interest in others   ❏ 8. Checking his stocks online

Compare your answers to those of the author in the Appendix.

CRITICAL CARRIE

A good manager listens carefully for critical facts and the logic that supports them. Critical listening is important in management, especially when solving problems. However, some managers listen in order to find fault.

Critical Carrie listens for the facts but is so critical of each item that she often misses the big picture. She seldom spends time with her staff, but when she does, she's usually issuing orders.

She asks abrupt questions and cuts people off before they can respond fully. Her questions are demanding and make her staff feel cornered. Carrie frowns or rolls her eyes in disbelief and is quick to place blame. Carrie is an incessant note-taker, so her eye contact is limited. She finds little time for small talk.

Her staff wishes she would lighten up and not jump to conclusions so quickly. Because she seldom listens to them, her staff members avoid her. Long ago, they stopped sharing information with her, because "she doesn't listen anyway."

What's Carrie's attitude?

_____

What would help Carrie communicate more effectively with her staff? Following is a list of behaviors. Put a check mark next to any that Carrie could adopt to improve her listening attitude.

❏ 1. Building rapport with small talk

❏ 2. Taking more notes

❏ 3. Listening for the "big picture"

❏ 4. Showing interest in employees

❏ 5. Creating an atmosphere of mistrust

❏ 6. Developing patience

❏ 7. Learning karate

❏ 8. Learning to smile

Compare your answers to those of the author in the Appendix.

COMPLIANT CURTIS

Compliant listening is a passive behavior that doesn't allow the speaker to understand the real feelings or opinions of the listener. Listeners such as Compliant Curtis listen much more than they talk. In many cases, they're shy. They want to please others and keep the conversation pleasant.

Compulsive blabbermouths often seek out listeners like Curtis, because they need someone with patience to listen to them.

Unfortunately, when Curtis speaks, he usually keeps his real opinions to himself for fear of criticism. Sometimes, he fakes attention as he silently thinks his private thoughts. In meetings, Curtis nods his head approvingly but adds little to the discussion. You'll recognize Compliant Curtis by such phrases as, "That's nice" or "I see your point."

What's Curtis' attitude?

_____

How can Curtis become a more involved listener? Put a check mark next to any of the following behaviors that would help him improve his listening style.

❑ 1. Listening with intention   ❑ 5. Daydreaming more often

❑ 2. Speaking with conviction   ❑ 6. Asking questions

❑ 3. Avoiding eye contact   ❑ 7. Voicing his opinions

❑ 4. Developing assertiveness   ❑ 8. Agreeing more often

Compare your answers to those of the author in the Appendix.

Bridges to Communication

Active listening is the bridge to good communication. It's committed listening based on good habits and self-control. Good listening is purposeful and productive, because it allows the listener and the speaker to reach a common understanding. Following are descriptions of active listening attitudes that create productive communication.

ARLO ACTIVE AND LISETTE LISTENER

Arlo Active, a skilled training director, is an involved listener. He's mentally present, he participates, and he assumes responsibility for the success of communications in his department. In meetings and discussions, Arlo requires discipline and relevance from his employees as he bridges gaps in understanding by asking questions for clarification.

He uses humor effectively to break tension and keep the agenda moving. Individuals in his department appreciate Arlo's clear verbal and nonverbal responses and focused eye contact. Arlo attempts to see other people's point of view, and he refrains from evaluating information too quickly. As an active listener, Arlo listens not only to the content of employees' statements, but also to their unspoken intent.

What's Arlo's attitude?

_____

Lisette Listener, a successful real estate agent, credits her success to purposeful listening. When interviewing potential clients, Lisette listens carefully to their requirements for a home. She pays close attention to where they want to live, their desired style of house, and the value they place on schools and services. She asks many questions for clarification. Then she feeds back what she hears to be sure she's accurate in her interpretation.

By the end of a busy day, Lisette often feels as tired as if she had built a house, rather than sold one. She realizes that active listening is hard work, but she knows her results are measured clearly by her commissions, her satisfied new home owners, and the new friends she makes.

What's Lisette's attitude?

_____

See the author's comments in the Appendix.

OTHER BRIDGES AND BARRIERS

What other listening attitudes (positive and negative) can you think of? What are some behaviors that support these attitudes?

Listening Attitude	Verbal or Nonverbal Behavior
Positive	
Negative	

How Well Do You Listen?

To find out how well you listen, take the following Personal Listening Inventory. It will help you to identify, plan, and practice the skills you need to improve your listening. The Personal Listening Inventory will help you to rate yourself as a listener. An interpretation of results follows the inventory. When you've completed it, you'll have a better insight into:

▶ How you rate yourself as a listener

▶ How you think others rate you as a listener

▶ How you rate others as listeners

PERSONAL LISTENING INVENTORY

1. On average, what percentage of each business day do you spend listening?

_____%

On a scale of 1-10 (with 10 being the highest)…

2. How would you rate yourself as a listener? _____

3. How committed are you to improving your listening? _____

4. How would you rate the best listener you know? _____

5. How would you rate the worst listener you know? _____

6. How would the following people (where appropriate) rate you as a listener?

▷ Your manager _____

▷ A subordinate _____

▷ Close colleague _____

▷ Spouse/significant other _____

▷ Your child(ren) _____

▷ Best friend _____

See the author's comments in the Appendix.

YOUR LISTENING QUALITIES: AN AWARENESS EXERCISE

List five of your best listening qualities, such as patience, good eye contact, not jumping to conclusions, asking for clarification, and others. Rank them 1-5, with 5 being the best quality.

1. _____
2. _____
3. _____
4. _____
5. _____

List three listening qualities that you don't have now but would like have.

1. _____
2. _____
3. _____

List five of your worst listening qualities, such as impatience, poor eye contact, jumping to conclusions, not asking for clarification, and others. Rank them 1-5 with 5 being the worst.

1. _____
2. _____
3. _____
4. _____
5. _____

Select one or more acquaintances and list three listening qualities of theirs that you'd like to avoid. Make a commitment to be more patient with those people and not fall into those behaviors yourself.

1. _____
2. _____
3. _____

How to Stop Bad Listening Habits

Bad habits aren't always easy to break. Following the suggestions below will help you stop those negative behaviors and replace them with something more desirable.

Catch yourself in the act

Recognition is the first step for preventive maintenance. On the previous page, you listed the listening habits you want to eliminate, so you can recognize them quickly. By monitoring your listening behavior, you can catch yourself when you fall into an undesirable habit, then take steps toward fixing it. Remember, you must want to change, or you won't make the effort.

Fight the habit

Don't tolerate what you want to eliminate. Stomp it. Drop it. Change your ways! Like a smoker kicking the habit, cold turkey is the best way. Don't wait until next time to do things differently. Admit your behavior (i.e., "I just interrupted you. I apologize. Please go on with what you were saying.") This is a way of catching yourself in the act and acknowledging your bad habit.

Replace the bad habit with a better one

Memorize the list of new habits you want to develop. If you're chronically impatient, learn patience. For example, think about how much you appreciate other people's patience when you're trying to explain something, then act the way you were treated. Visualize yourself as patient, or not interrupting, or listening without daydreaming. Look for the value in the new behavior you choose and trust yourself to do it.

Acknowledge your success

When you substitute an improved listening behavior successfully, give yourself a reward or a pat on the back. Put money toward a vacation fund, or a star in your listening diary. Say to yourself, "I did it!" Tell someone, to see if he or she praises you; better yet, tell someone you *know* will praise you.

Be patient with yourself. Why is it that we're more tolerant of other people's mistakes than of our own? Cut yourself some slack. In other words, give yourself a break, and be realistic when you set your goals. Self-improvement is a lifelong project, and the road to success is always under construction. There's no such thing as perfect listening, but we can all do better.

How to Help Someone Listen to You

Much of this book focuses on how you can become a better listener. And although your skills may improve, how do you help others improve their skills? How do you get them to listen to you? If only there were better news here.

The hard truth is that we can be responsible only for our own listening. If we listen respectfully and model good listening behavior, we're more likely to be heard. However, some people aren't attentive listeners, despite your good example. In this case, be assertive and ask them to listen. Ask politely and with good will. If you don't mention the problem, chances are that they'll continue to listen haphazardly, because poor listeners usually don't know they're doing anything wrong. They're both unskilled and uninformed.

Statements to Help People Listen:

"I feel that I'm not being listened to (heard)."

"This information is important, and I want to know that you're hearing me. So I need your undivided attention."

"Please listen to me."

"I feel (ignored, angry, unimportant to you) when you don't listen."

"Let me repeat what I just said, as it's important that you hear it."

"I need for you to hear this, so please let me finish what I'm saying."

Behaviors That Will Help People Listen to You

Following are suggestions that may make it easier for others to want to listen to you. Place a check mark next to those you identify with.

❑ **I'm interested in the thoughts and opinions of others.**

People don't care what you know until they know you care. Don't expect others to listen to you, if you're heedless, impatient, or overly critical. Respect must be mutual for good communication to thrive.

❑ **I'm interesting to talk to.**

I have a few hobbies, go to the movies, read the paper, or like sports. I know what's happening on television, the Internet, and I twitter/tweet. I've traveled. I tell good stories, and I know a few jokes appropriate for mixed audiences. I speak clearly and distinctly, and I use good English. I don't repeat myself. I don't sprinkle my vocabulary with colorful epithets (swearing). I have one or two areas of expertise about which I can speak with some authority (gardening, computers, raising dogs, and others). I'm enthusiastic. I don't speak in a monotone or sound bored. If I'm shy, I try to believe in myself and express my opinions more often. (If you feel that others wouldn't be interested in hearing what you have to say because you're a little boring, take a Dale Carnegie course. It can't hurt.)

❑ **I tell the truth.**

Remember the old adage, "If you tell the truth, you won't have to remember what you said." Everybody has a good "baloney barometer," and exaggeration and white lies are seldom tolerated for long.

❑ **I avoid "bigshotitis" and name-dropping.**

Familiar references to famous people or high-ranking officials are appropriate, if we know them well. Otherwise, we're using their names to make ourselves look important. Putting ourselves in a "one-up" position means that the listener is in a "one-down" position. Then communication becomes competition.

❑ **I'm my authentic self.**

You're the first-best you and the second-best anyone else. Being comfortable with being you is the greatest gift you can give yourself. You're unique. Let that be enough. Pretense is a result of trying to be like someone else, because we don't like who we are. When we're settled with ourselves, others find us more approachable and likable.

❑ **I'm conscious of timing and preliminary tuning.**

I prepare my listener for what I'm going to say. For example: "You should know the counts for both kinds of cholesterol when your cholesterol level is tested. Let me say why I think that." Be aware of the processing time needed by your listener. Be patient. Some people are internal processors and take extra time to think before they respond. External processors may answer rapidly, but they might not respond as clearly or accurately.

❑ **I get to the point and keep the message moving.**

Too much detail kills interest. Keep your listener stimulated by providing new ideas and adding colorful words, anecdotes, and visual images. Avoid jargon, clichés, and hackneyed phrases. Be specific and be clear. Don't repeat yourself. Don't force assumptions. Fill in the background, but avoid endless detail. When possible, plan what you'll say to make it easy for the listener.

❑ **I'm sensitive to my listener's needs.**

Don't drop verbal grenades when the listener is in the wrong physical or psychological state. Break bad news gently. It isn't what you say, but how you say it. Outline your message. "Our financial picture is somewhat bleak for next quarter. Here are three ideas for coping with the problem." Say the vital parts first and last. People seldom remember what's in the middle.

❑ **I use my listener's name regularly.**

People love to hear their own names. Use them often in your communication, but use good judgment. If you use them too often, you sound rehearsed and insincere (or like you've just read a book about communication skills).

❑ **I use good eye communication.**

Really seeing people is very different from just looking at them. Use eye contact and other nonverbal behaviors as signals to your listeners that you want to talk with them, rather than at them. Be conscious of the speaker's eye contact and use about the same amount that he or she does. Use this knowledge to establish a level of comfort between you. Our eye contact, personal attitudes, habits, and intentions greatly affect the way we listen to others.

Part Summary

In this part, you learned that a **listening attitude** is your key to success. Next, you learned some **barriers** to communication, followed by some **bridges** to communication. You learned **how well you listen**. Then, you learned how to **stop bad listening habits**. Finally, you learned how to **help someone listen** to you.

Points to Remember

▶ Attitude is a choice.

▶ Positive and negative listening behavior starts with attitude.

▶ Most people aren't good listeners.

▶ We listen best when there's a payoff or a penalty.

▶ Personal listening awareness is the key to constructive change.

Ten Tips For
Tip-Top Listening

"*As friends we don't see eye to eye, but then we don't hear ear to ear either.*"

—Buster Keaton

In this part:

Listen Louder

Listening is both a behavior and a skill. Behavior is evidence of our ability to apply a skill. To improve our listening skills we need to practice consciously the ten tips in this section. A good driver does more than simply avoid accidents, and a good listener does more than simply pay attention.

Because business is a place where you must listen most of the time, you'll have plenty of opportunity to practice. Mentally condition yourself to make every encounter, from your first phone call to the last meeting of the day, an opportunity to practice improved listening. Be practical and select the tips that will help you the most.

The following tips will help you "listen louder." Consciously select those you wish to work on, then establish a list of listening priorities.

Tip 1: Take Notes

Good listeners are note-takers. They realize that minds are imprecise and memory is imperfect. Note-taking helps you follow disorganized speakers, locate the key points, and identify supporting data. The following suggestions can help you to improve your note-taking skills.

Be prepared. Carry a small notepad and a pen at all times. Some people prefer a tape recorder or a laptop instead. Use your note-taking tools regularly to record any thoughts or ideas you want to remember. Note the speaker, the situation, and the time. In selected situations, you should ask permission before you take notes, use your laptop, or record information. Use good judgment.

Get it down. Don't take time to be overly neat. If necessary, you can recopy your notes later. Write just clearly enough so you remember what you wrote and why. Answer the questions: who? what? where? when? and why?

Don't try to write everything. Avoid complete sentences. Write nouns that create visual pictures. Use active verbs. Develop your own shorthand, including symbols, pictures, punctuation, and abbreviations (e.g., Suzie Hilgeman, lnch w/ HP client, Fri. 11:30 @ Jo Jo's). Be sure to get the correct spelling of people's names.

"I'd tell you everything but I hear you charge by the word."

Tip 2: Listen Now, Report Later

You can improve your listening significantly by planning to report what you heard to someone later. Taking notes increases your effectiveness even more. Think of a co-worker or a friend who'd benefit from or enjoy the information you're listening to, and plan to tell him or her what you've learned. Your listening then takes on the added dimension of a rehearsal.

Tip 3: Want to Listen

To be a good listener, we must be willing to give up a preoccupation with ourselves. Simply put, we must want to listen. The following memory device describes the skills and attitudes we need to insure our listening success.

To be a good listener, use your DISC drive.

Desire. From a desire to listen comes a commitment. A committed athlete doesn't play half of each game. A committed gardener doesn't water just half of the garden. We must have a strong desire to listen in order to be effective communicators. Listening isn't a halfway process.

Interest. According to the writer G.K. Chesterton, there's no such thing as an uninteresting topic; there are just uninterested people. We must develop an interest in the person and/or in the topic to be good listeners.

Self-discipline. We must learn self-discipline to eliminate distractions, understand the speaker's key points, overcome boredom, interpret voice inflections and tone, understand nonverbal cues, and comprehend the main idea. Next time you're in a listening situation, pay attention to how well you control your negative listening habits.

Concentration. Concentration requires greater effort than does merely paying attention. You pay attention when you juggle balls, and you concentrate when you juggle eggs. Concentration is focused mental energy, and it's a limited commodity. How long can you concentrate intently in a meeting or on your cell phone (especially if you're driving)? Why can some people concentrate for hours, while others grow restless in minutes? Think of concentration as money in the bank. For most of us, money is a limited resource. You must discipline yourself to spend it carefully. You must choose how to spend your concentration energy as well.

You have more ability to concentrate at some times than at others. Are you more alert in the morning or in the afternoon? How well do you concentrate after a heavy meal or a hard day on the job? Take advantage of your maximum ability to concentrate by:

▶ Planning your time

▶ Knowing your limits

▶ Setting listening priorities

To improve your concentration, develop an opportunistic attitude. Ask yourself these questions:

▶ Why am I listening?

▶ What can I learn that I can pass along to someone else?

▶ How can I use this information?

Concentration improves when you develop mental pictures of what the speaker is saying. If Joe calls to say that he'll have the Wilson report on your desk by 2:30 P.M. on Friday, visualize Joe placing the report on your desk. Notice how Joe is dressed. Imagine the word Wilson in bold letters on the cover of the report. See, in your mind, a clock that reads 2:30 P.M. next to your desk calendar turned to Friday.

You can exaggerate any of these mental images, such as giving Joe a clown's nose, or Wilson written in purple Crayola to enhance your mental image. By visualizing what you want to remember, you create "dwell time" for your mind to encode the information into long-term storage.

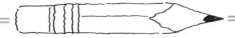

LISTENING LAB: CONCENTRATION CHECKLIST

Complete this exercise to identify some reasons why you don't always concentrate. Rate items that apply to you using a scale from 0-3, with 0 being no problem; 1 being a minor problem; 2 being somewhat of a problem; and 3 being a major problem. Compare your total to the table at the end of the exercise.

_____ I'm in a hurry.

_____ I become distracted by what's going on around me.

_____ I'm self-conscious.

_____ I'm bored.

_____ I'm thinking about what I'm going to say next.

_____ I'm in surroundings that are out of my comfort zone.

_____ I already know what the speaker is going to say.

_____ I'm used to having things repeated.

_____ I'm on mental overload most of the time.

_____ I'm not responsible for the information.

_____ I'm tired.

_____ I'm confused by the topic or the speaker.

_____ I'm daydreaming.

_____ **TOTAL**

0 to 3: You have excellent concentration skills.
4 to 8: This book should help to improve your concentration skills.
9+: You need a specific action plan to improve concentration skills. And you probably need a vacation.

Tip 4: Stop Daydreaming

Like it or not, we always choose whether or not we'll listen. When we choose not to listen, our minds are on holiday, and we don't interpret, evaluate, or respond appropriately to the speaker and the message. Only when we choose to be present are we focused on the speaker and the message.

Our number one alternative to being present is daydreaming. Daydreaming is a comfortable private escape. Normally, it doesn't disturb anyone, and often others don't realize we're doing it Daydreaming is what we elect to do when we choose not to listen.

Daydreaming is the single greatest barrier to active listening. To be present and listen effectively, we must recognize our mental truancies, put them aside, and bring ourselves back to the subject at hand.

The following exercise will help you recognize your Daydream Quotient (DQ.)

LISTENING LAB: CHECK YOUR DQ

For this exercise, take a piece of paper and make note of any time you daydream while listening to your instructor or reading the rest of this book. If your mind wanders, jot down where it went and what you were thinking, then quickly return your attention to listening or reading.

When you complete this course, review your DQ to see if you find repeated subjects or patterns in your daydreams. If so, they may be matters for conscious attention and action.

We All Daydream

We all daydream—many of us as much as 50 percent of the time. Next time you're in a listening situation, check your DQ to notice how often you wander off mentally while the speaker is talking. Do you think about what you're going to say next? If you wander at least once per minute, chances are you need more concentration and self-discipline in your listening.

Effective listeners focus on the speaker and listen hard for the content of the message. They avoid the embarrassment of being caught daydreaming. While we're never tested on our daydreams, we can, at any time, be tested on the content of the message.

By the way, if you find yourself thinking about what you'll say when it's your turn to talk, set the thought aside. If it's important, you'll remember it later.

Tip 5: Anticipate Excellence

Expectations play a powerful role in our lives. How often do we avoid a co-worker because we don't want to listen to small talk? We just know it would be boring. Other times, we may have skipped a lecture, because it would be too intellectual.

By giving others a chance to speak intelligently and by anticipating excellence from them, we can help them become successful. As humans, we have a deep need to be heard and understood. When we set aside our needs and truly listen, people drop their pretenses and speak to us in a more mature and connected manner.

Listeners can help speakers by:

▶ Asking questions   ▶ Expressing concern

▶ Showing interest   ▶ Paying attention

CASE STUDY: The Pioneer's Story

This story is about pioneers in covered wagons crossing the Oregon Territory. They stopped to rest at a small settlement, and the wagon master spoke to an old man sunning himself in front of the general store.

"Say, old timer, what kind of people have settled out here?"

"What kind of people were they where you came from?" asked the old man.

"Well, they were mean, full of mischief, and small-minded. That's why we left," replied the wagon master.

"Sorry, young feller, that's the kind of folks you find here," said the old man.

Later in the week, another wagon train pulled into the town for supplies. This wagon master also stopped in front of the general store and spoke to the same old man. "Say, friend, what kind of people have settled here?"

"What kind of people were they where you came from?" asked the old man.

"The people we left behind were kind, decent people, and they were generous. When we left, they gave us supplies and helped us load our wagons."

"Well, my friend, you've come to the right place, because those are the kind of folks you'll find out here," replied the old man with a kindly smile.

We get what we expect! Anticipate excellence, and it will happen a lot more often than if we assume otherwise.

Tip 6: Become a "Whole Body" Listener

To be an effective listener, involve your whole body. Not only are our ears tuned in, but so are our eyes, our minds (the intellect), our bodies, our hearts, and our intuition. Good listeners give both verbal and nonverbal signals that they;re listening.

A "whole body" listener tunes in by:

- ▶ Conveying a positive, encouraging attitude
- ▶ Sitting in an attentive posture
- ▶ Remaining alert, but comfortable
- ▶ Nodding in acknowledgment of the speaker's words
- ▶ Making good eye contact
- ▶ Listening between the lines
- ▶ Looking like a listener

If you have complete rapport, you'll naturally match the speaker's physical movements, tone of voice, vocabulary, and breathing patterns. Good listeners are in sensory balance with the speaker.

According to Albert Mehrabian, a noted expert in human behavior, our communication is 55 percent nonverbal, 38 percent inflection and tone, and only 7 percent words.

If Mehrabian is correct, then most of the spoken message is seen and sensed, and the words are far less important than the nonverbal cues and tone of voice.

Think about your personal mannerisms and behaviors. Do you have any of the following habits that would distract or confuse a speaker?

Twitching and fidgeting	Playing with your hair, tie, or jewelry
Blinking	Looking at your watch
Biting your lip or nails	Frowning deeply
Staring	

Stop a moment and think about these behaviors. Would they distract you if you were the one speaking? If your answer is yes, you need to find a way to modify your behavior. Try the suggestions in the following exercise.

LISTENING LAB:
BECOMING A "WHOLE BODY" LISTENER

1. Check Your Habits

Briefly write your nonverbal listening responses toward two people you know. Choose one person you enjoy and one person you don't. Are your responses different? If so, how? If you want to change any of your nonverbal responses to either person, use the Change column to state your improvement goal.

Person #1

Response	Description	Change
Posture		
Eye contact		
Facial expression		
Mannerisms		
General attitude		
Voice (verbal response)		

Person #2

Response	Description	Change
Posture		
Eye contact		
Facial expression		
Mannerisms		
General attitude		
Voice (verbal response)		

CONTINUED

2. Consider Nonverbal Encouragement

List five things you can do nonverbally to encourage a speaker.

1. _____

2. _____

3. _____

4. _____

5. _____

Tip 7: Build Rapport by Pacing the Speaker

Pacing is a method listeners use to build a positive relationship with a speaker by imitating or mirroring his or her verbal and nonverbal cues. These cues include breathing, voice rate, vocabulary, favorite phrases, facial expressions, and general body language. Of course, if we imitate too closely, we'll be accused of mimicking, and our attempts to build rapport will be lost.

When pacing, the listener focuses on what the speaker is doing as well as on what he or she is saying. The listener then attempts to become more like the speaker. The speaker senses the similarities and feels at ease, because we're more comfortable with people who are more like us. When others' behaviors are very different from our own, we adjust less easily to their styles.

This technique isn't meant to manipulate. If your intention is to build rapport, you can do it more easily if you take your attention away from yourself and focus it on the other person. That's the purpose of pacing.

As a listener, you can pace those speaking in any of the following ways:

▶ Match your voice rate to the speaker's. Speed up or slow down as necessary.

▶ Change your voice volume to match the speaker's.

▶ Notice and use some of the same words and phrases the speaker does.

▶ Approximate the speaker's gestures. Sit forward or back, hands on or off the desk, etc. Don't be too obvious, or you'll be noticed. Approximate the gestures.

▶ Breathe at about the same rate, without being too obvious. (If the speaker is a Type A and breathes very fast, be careful not to hyperventilate.)

CASE STUDY: Cheryl's Story

Cheryl was preparing to give a technical speech before a large, important audience. She arrived early at the meeting room to check her PowerPoint presentation and adapt to the circumstances of the room. When she set up her computer, she discovered that her power cord was missing. She had no replacement in her computer case.

Frantically, she searched the building for a maintenance person. She found the maintenance supervisor on the next floor, ambling slowly down the hall. Cheryl rushed to the supervisor, explaining her dilemma in a rapid staccato voice that displayed obvious urgency.

Bill, the supervisor, was low-keyed. While Cheryl churned like a buzz saw, Bill spoke no faster than a snail on Valium. Cheryl felt she could count to 10 between each of Bill's words. "I'd – like – to – help – you, – but – I – left – the – key – to- the – supply – closet – on – my – desk," said Bill in a low, slow, patient monotone. Cheryl continued to buzz and Bill continued to dawdle for another minute.

Suddenly Cheryl remembered something she'd read about pacing, and she decided to give it a try. Gradually, she began to slow her speech to match Bill's rate. It was painful for Cheryl to talk so slowly, but Bill became more responsive and helpful as she became less frantic.

Within minutes, Bill remembered someone who had a key, and he volunteered to find the cord she needed. Cheryl couldn't be sure the pacing made the difference, but within 15 minutes, she had the replacement cord. Bill flashed a big slow smile as he handed her the cord, along with a spare, in case the replacement didn't work. Cheryl thanked Bill s-l-o-w-l-y and smiled back. She'd found a new and important friend.

CASE STUDY: Byron's Story

Byron was a representative for a refrigeration company in Texas. Because of his large territory, he made most of his contacts by phone. Byron had heard of pacing from a friend and decided to try it in his cold calls and follow-up calls.

When he called potential customers, he listened carefully to what they said and how they said it. Then, as he spoke, he paced their voices, speed, inflection, and vocabulary. With no changes other than listening and pacing, Byron was able to increase his equipment sales by 20 percent over the previous quarter.

LISTENING LAB: PACING THE SPEAKER

To develop an ability to pace effectively, follow these guidelines in the suggested sequence:

1. Practice pacing with a friend. First, tell him or her what you're doing. Have your friend tell you a funny story or describe an interesting place to visit while using varied gestures and facial expressions. Mirror each action and expression to get the feeling for the pacing activity. When both of you stop laughing, discuss how successful you were and solicit suggestions for improvement.

2. Next, practice pacing on a friend or family member in a no-risk situation. This time try to remain undetected.

3. Finally, practice on a colleague, choosing one or two characteristics to mirror. Be natural and sincere. As you pace and observe, exhibit an attitude of wanting to build rapport.

Rapport is the ultimate tool in producing positive results with others. In business, dealing effectively with people is essential. Rapport can help us achieve success. We build rapport by listening actively and acting on what we hear.

84

Tip 8: Control Emotional Hot-Buttons

Words, issues, situations, and personalities trigger us emotionally. When these issues trigger our emotional hot-buttons, verbal messages become distorted, either positively or negatively. Emotional issues can create barriers to effective listening. When our hot-buttons are activated, we tune out, distort, or prejudge these emotionally charged messages.

Emotional hot-buttons are intense, complex feelings that affect everyone. Each may initiate a different emotional reaction, but our physical responses are similar. If you can't eliminate your emotional hot-buttons, the best alternative is to develop acceptable responses. The physical triggers warn you that emotions are taking over. When emotional levels go up, objectivity comes down. Problems are never resolved satisfactorily at an emotional level.

To control emotional hot-buttons, we must identify what triggers us, understand our responses, and develop behaviors that allow us to listen more carefully and objectively. The following method can help you identify your listening hot-buttons.

LISTENING LAB: IDENTIFYING HOT-BUTTONS

Step 1

Following are some listening situations and phrases that may cause you to become emotional. Place a check mark next to those that are hot-buttons for you as a listener, and add others that affect you strongly, positively or negatively.

- ❏ "You never/always…"
- ❏ Know-it-all attitudes
- ❏ "Shut up!"
- ❏ Bad grammar
- ❏ "It's your fault."

- ❏ Pushy people
- ❏ Cell phone addicts
- ❏ Whining
- ❏ "What you should do is…"
- ❏ Texting

Your favorites:

_____

_____

_____

CONTINUED

The Business of Listening

CONTINUED

Step 2

Read through the list again and cross out any hot-button issues you're willing to give up, in other words, those you can forget and not let them bother you again. Chances are you won't cross off many items from your list. This step shows that it's difficult to give up habitual ways of responding to emotional situations.

Step 3

Put a check mark next to the responses on the following list that describes your physical reactions to emotionally charged issues:

❏ Can't think   ❏ Chest tightens

❏ Heartbeat increases   ❏ Feel faint

❏ Hands feel sweaty   ❏ Lose appetite

❏ Voice shakes   ❏ Get hysterical

Others: _____

_____

_____

Ten Steps for Controlling Emotional Hot-Buttons

Following is a list of coping skills for preventive maintenance when your hot-buttons are activated.

1. Listen attentively without interrupting. Take deep breaths to help you control your physical reactions.

2. Make a conscious choice about your response. You can get angry, try to solve the problem, or ignore it. If you choose to solve the problem, you can prevent it from happening again.

3. Acknowledge other people's feelings. Make it okay for them to feel the way they do.

4. Ask objective questions for clarification. Open-ended questions are useful.

5. Try to see the other person's point of view. Agree where you can, and feed back what you're hearing.

6. Stick to the subject. Define the problem and don't let other issues interfere.

7. Be patient. Problems don't always have immediate solutions. Be patient with the other person—and yourself.

8. Express your point of view. Don't force proof. Present your evidence without backing the other person into a corner.

9. Explain why. A reasonable explanation can often take the sting out of emotional issues.

10. Work out a win-win plan, usually a compromise. Make sure your solution is fair and workable for everyone involved.

LISTENING LAB: PREVENTIVE MAINTENANCE FOR EMOTIONAL HOT-BUTTONS

In the first column below, list three people who affect you emotionally when you listen to them. Next, write down the hot-button issue that activates your reaction to each of them. Finally, develop a preventive-maintenance plan to control or modify your emotional reaction.

Person	Hot-button	Preventive Maintenance
1.		
2.		
3.		

Tip 9: Control Distractions

Comedian George Carlin once asked, "Aren't you glad the phone wasn't invented by Alexander Graham Siren?" Telephones and cell phones are some of the biggest distractions to listening in a business environment, because unseen others choose when the phone rings. If the phone were the only distraction, we could probably tolerate it. Every day, however, we must deal with many internal, external, and auditory distractions.

To be good listeners, we must control our responses to distractions or they control us. Distractions affect the ability to listen well because of their variety, novelty, and intensity. External distractions include the telephone, background noise, unfamiliar vocabulary, seating, lighting, and many others. Internal distractions might be headaches, hunger, fatigue, illness, or a current emotional state, such as anxiety.

CASE STUDY: Stephanie's Story

Stephanie was putting the finishing touches on a major marketing presentation when a colleague called to discuss a budget problem. Stephanie automatically grabbed the phone and answered while still assembling binders. Suddenly she realized her distraction. She told her colleague politely that she was just finishing a project with a tight deadline. She asked if she could return the call in an hour, when the project was finished, so that she could be a better listener. By handling the matter this way, Stephanie avoided distraction. She let the caller know of her desire to give the budget problem her full attention as soon as possible.

Life and work are full of distractions. Our professional responsibility is to manage our environment. Although working conditions are never ideal, we can minimize distractions by taking action to improve our listening, which helps to reduce communication problems.

LISTENING LAB: OVERCOMING DISTRACTIONS

The following statements describe how people might handle various distractions. Place a check mark next to those items you do well.

❑ **Plan your listening.** Don't attempt important business in a restaurant or a bar. It's too noisy, and you're interrupted frequently. Find a quiet room and turn off your cell phone or pager for important meetings. Plan decision-making meetings during your high-energy times of the day. Think beforehand about possible distractions and plan to avoid them if you can.

❑ **Agree with others to eliminate distractions.** By recognizing that distractions may occur, you and your colleagues can agree ahead of time to turn off cell phones, get coffee before you start, and set expectations (agenda, time, breaks, necessary interruptions) in order to minimize distractions.

❑ **Don't use distractions as a convenient excuse for not listening.** Overcome distractions with extra determination and concentration.

❑ **Identify what's causing a distraction and make adjustments.** Are you too near a noisy copier? Can you move away from it? Do you have a headache? Have you taken an aspirin? Are you hungry? Can you eat an apple? Are the lights too low or too high? Can they be adjusted? Is the phone a problem? Can someone else take your calls? In other words, when you've identified the problem, you're one step closer to fixing it.

❑ **Ignore the distraction.** If you can't do anything about the street repairs outside your window, tune them out by concentrating harder. Although you know the distraction is there, focus your attention on the speaker. Use self-discipline.

❑ **Call "time out" when you're too tired to listen.** Audial fatigue is caused by constant noise, such as humming fans, droning traffic, or a grumbling stomach. Intense concentration or physical exhaustion can also cause "ear exhaustion." Don't be shy about calling a recess when you've had enough noise.

Tip 10: Listening Is a Gift—Give Generously!

Listening is a skill that anyone can learn. It's also a gift that anyone can give. It's a special gift of a person's time and attention. Listening is an acknowledgment of caring. Honest listening encourages a speaker to be creative and feel more accepted.

The gift of listening assumes that the speaker has value, dignity, and something to offer. We listen every day. If, in our listening, we take the focus off ourselves and encourage the speaker to express his or her ideas, we extend a gift that will be repaid many times. Develop a listening attitude. The results are worth it.

A Gift of Listening

This certificate entitles you to one-half-hour of my undivided attention. I'll listen to you carefully and thoughtfully. I won't interrupt, and I'll ask questions only for clarification.

_____

Listener

Part Summary

In this part, you learned how to **listen louder** by using listening tips. First, you learned how to **take notes** while listening. Then, you learned to **plan a report** of what you've heard. Next, you learned that you must **want to listen**. You learned to **stop daydreaming** and **anticipate excellence**. Then, you learned to become a **"whole body" listener** and to build rapport by **pacing the speaker**. You learned the value of **controlling emotional hot-buttons** and **distractions**. Finally, you learned how to give the **gift** of listening.

Points to Remember

▶ Take notes. They aid retention.

▶ Listen now, report later. Plan to tell someone what you heard; you'll remember it better.

▶ Want to listen. You must have desire, interest, self-discipline, and concentration to be a good listener.

▶ Be present. Watch out for the tendency to daydream.

▶ Anticipate excellence. We get good information more often when we expect it.

▶ Become a "whole-body" listener. Listen with your ears, your eyes, your heart, your intuition, and your mind.

▶ Build rapport by pacing the speaker. Approximate the speaker's gestures, expressions, and voice patterns to create comfortable communication.

▶ Control your emotional "hot buttons." Knowing what makes you react emotionally is your key to preventive maintenance.

▶ Control distractions. Controlling internal and external distractions helps you manage your working environment effectively.

▶ Give the gift of listening. Listening is a skill—and a gift. Give generously and give often.

A P P E N D I X

Develop a Personal Action Plan

A definition of accountability is to be responsible for one's actions. We all have good intentions. What separates those who are successful from those who aren't is how well we carry out those intentions. This Personal Action Plan can convert your good intentions into actions. It's a good starting point if you're serious about improving your listening skills.

1. My current listening skills are effective in the following areas:

2. I need to improve my listening skills in the following areas:

3. I'll implement an action plan for listening improvement as follows:

    a. My listening goals:

    b. My plan for reaching my goals:

    c. My timetable:

4. The following person(s) will benefit from my improved listening skills:

5. They'll benefit in the following ways:

Appendix to Part 1

Comments & Suggested Responses

The Benefits of Listening

1. **T.** Being a good listener will help you to make better informed decisions.

2. **T.** Whether people have an axe to grind, or just need a shoulder to lean on, the one thing most people need is someone to listen to them.

3. **T.** Good listeners get the instructions right the first time, and are often able to do more work in less time than their peers.

4. **T.** Listening will help you to better understand someone else's position. And being listened to will often help an antagonist to calm down.

5. **T.** Good listeners are rarely told, "You don't understand the issue," after making a response.

6. **F.** After absorbing all the facts, good listeners are able to say a lot that others want to hear.

7. **T.** Clients don't like having to repeat themselves, and they like it when things are done right the first time.

8. **F.** Good listeners make good leaders.

9. **T.** Good listeners are better problem solvers than poor listeners.

10. **F.** Good listeners learn how to separate the information fron the noise.

What Do You Know about Listening?

1. **F.** Facts are only part of most messages. Good listeners listen for opinion, emotion, and distortion as well.

2. **T.** To listen well, open your eyes, use your brain, your heart, and your intuition.

3. **T.** Hearing is the first step, but you must also interpret, evaluate, and respond to the message.

4. **F.** Paying attention is important, but it's only the first step. You must be able to understand and respond to the message, and you must care about the person and/or the message as well.

5. **F.** Many people pride themselves on being able to multitask, but the more you try to do at the same time, the more you scatter your attention. Good listening is focused attention.

6. **T.** Your body and mind and spirit work together. If your body is slumped and lumpy, it gives your mind and spirit the same signals. Remember your parents' and teachers' admonition: "Sit up straight and listen!"

7. **T.** Most can, but not all. If you're distracted, mention it, move, or do something about it. When that doesn't work, ignore the distraction.

8. **F.** Yes, memory is an overlay of listening, but you may need to remember something for only a short time. We can't consciously remember everything we've heard in the past, but if we were able to listen and act on the information effectively at the time, we were listening.

9. **F.** Listening is anything but passive. Your eyes dilate, your palms perspire, and your body is erect. Your mind is active and your energy is focused.

10. **F.** If the speaker says something you don't understand, interrupt politely and ask for clarification. Otherwise, you'll lose the meaning of what follows. Taking notes helps.

Appendix to Part 2

Comments & Suggested Responses

Listening Lab 1: Hearing the Message

1. We hear sounds constantly, but remember few of them.

2. We remember sounds that are important, interesting, or unusual.

3. Same as #2

4. We all daydream frequently. We can't remember what we didn't hear.

5. People complain sometimes that they can't listen as well when they aren't wearing their glasses, because they can't see the speaker's nonverbal message.

Appendix to Part 4

Comments & Suggested Responses

Vacant Vincent

Attitude: "I don't want to be involved."

Answers: 1, 2, 4, 5, 6

Critical Carrie

Attitude: "I know all the answers."

Answers: 1, 3, 4, 6, 8

Compliant Curtis

Attitude: "I don't want to be criticized."

Answers: 1, 2, 4, 6, 7

Arlo Active and Lisette Listener

Arlo's Attitude: Effective listening is important to me and to my job.

Lisette's Attitude: Effective listening pays big dividends.

Personal Listening Inventory

The following comments on the Personal Listening Inventory will help you compare your results with those of others.

1. According to experts, we spend approximately 80 percent of each business day communicating. Of that time, 45 percent is spent listening, 30 percent speaking, 16 percent reading, and 9 percent writing. A manager or a student may spend up to 60 percent of each day listening.

2. Most people listen at about 50 percent efficiency. In other words, if tested immediately on what they just heard, they'd remember about 50 percent of it. However, the efficiency rate drops off quickly, and most people average a rate of 25 percent overall.

3. This is a biggie! We need to commit to becoming better listeners, because listening is hard work. It requires attention, patience, persistence, and a plan for improvement. Casual involvement and genuine commitment aren't the same thing. Suppose you had ham and eggs for breakfast. The chicken was involved in your breakfast, but the pig was committed. What's your commitment to your listening improvement?

4. Best listeners are usually rated as 8, 9, or 10. This is higher than most individuals rate themselves. The best listeners are often mentors, role models, or professional counselors.

5. Worst listeners are usually rated as 0-4. The score is much lower than most people rate themselves. "Worst listeners" are often related to us, probably because we save our worst behaviors for the people closest to us.

6. It isn't unusual to discover that our best friends rate us highest, and our family lowest. Subordinates and colleagues rank us about the same as we rank ourselves. Bosses usually rank us higher than we rank ourselves, because we listen better to them than we do to others. In other words, we're more attentive when there's a direct payoff—or penalty.

Additional Reading

Crisp 50-Minute Series books:

Bozek, Phillip E. *50 One Minute Tips to Better Communication*.

Decker, Bert. *The Art of Communicating*.

Other related reading:

Burley-Allen, Madelyn. *Listening: The Forgotten Skill (Self-Teaching Guide)*. New York, NY: John Wiley & Sons, 1995.

Burley-Allen, Madelyn. *Listening: The Forgotten Skill (Audiobook MP3-Unabridged)*. New York: Gildan Media Corp., 2008

Condrill, Jo and Bennie Bough. *101 Ways to Improve Your Communication Skills*. Beverly Hills, CA: Goal Minds, 1999.

Connaught Hall Senior Members' Handbook: Listening Skills. www.scribd.com/doc. 1 June 2009.

Devereaux, Rochelle. *Power Listening (audio cassette)*. Salem, OR: Business Efficacy, 1997.

Downs, Lisa. (ital.) *Listening Skills Training* (ASTD Trainer's Workshop Series), Washington DC: ASTD Press, 2008.

James, Art, and Robinson-Kratz, Abby. *Effective Listening Skills*. New York: McGraw-Hill Companies. 1995

Powell-Smith, Michelle. *Learning Active Listening Skills*. How To. 16 July 2009 www.ehow.com

Winzurk, Judith. *Quick Skills: Listening*. Career Solutions Training Group, Ohio: South-Western Educational Pub, 2000.

50-Minute™ Series

If you enjoyed this book, we have great news for you.
There are more than 200 books available in the
Crisp Fifty-Minute™ Series.

Subject Areas Include:

Management and Leadership
Human Resources
Communication Skills
Personal Development
Sales and Marketing
Accounting and Finance
Coaching and Mentoring
Customer Service/Quality
Small Business and Entrepreneurship
Writing and Editing

For more information visit us online at

www.CrispSeries.com

VERS

Get the ebook FREE!

To get a free PDF copy of this book
(sold separately for $27.50) purchase the print
book and register it at the Manning website
following the instructions inside this insert.

That's it!

Thanks from Manning!